W9-CHU-789

Library of the

oceans

Library of the
oceans

the world's oceans

GROLIER EDUCATIONAL
SHERMAN TURNPIKE, DANBURY, CONNECTICUT 06816

551.46
J LIB

Published 1998 by Grolier Educational
Sherman Turnpike, Danbury, Connecticut.
Copyright © 1998 Marshall Cavendish Limited

All rights in this book are reserved. No part of this book may be used or reproduced in any manner whatsoever or transmitted in any form or by any means, electronic or mechanical, including photocopying, recording, or any information storage and retrieval system, without written permission from the copyright owner except in the case of brief quotations embodied in critical articles and reviews. For information, address the publisher:
Grolier Educational, Sherman Turnpike, Danbury,
Connecticut 06816

Set ISBN : 0-7172-9180-4
Volume ISBN : 0-7172-9190-1

Library of the oceans.
p.   cm.
Includes bibliographical references and index.
Contents: v. 1. The shape of the oceans -- v. 2. The restless waters -- v. 3. The prehistoric ocean --
v. 4. Life in the ocean -- v. 5. Hunters and monsters -- v. 6. The cold seas -- v. 7. The warm seas --
v. 8. The shallow seas -- v. 9. Exploring the oceans -- v. 10. The world's oceans --
v. 11. Coasts and islands -- v. 12. The future of the ocean.
ISBN 0-7172-9180-4 (set). – ISBN 0-7172-9190-1 (v. 10).
1. Oceanography – Juvenile literature. [1. Ocean. 2. Oceanography.]   I. Grolier Educational Corporation.
GC21.5.L33   1998   97-42835
551.46–dc21   CIP
                                                                                                              AC

Marshall Cavendish Limited
Editorial staff
Managing editor: Ellen Dupont
Project editor: Tim Cooke
Editors: Andrew Brown, Sarah Halliwell, Tessa Paul
Assistant editor: Lorien Kite
Senior designer: Richard Newport
Designers: Christopher McDonald, Joyce Mason, Louise Morley, Richard Shiner
Picture administration/editorial assistant: Darren Brasher
Text: Alice Peebles
Consultants: Dr. Stuart Evans, University of Leeds
Dr. Carolyn Heeps, University of Bournemouth
Dr. Barbara Ransom, Scripps Institution of Oceanography
Index: Ann Hall
Production: Craig Chubb, Jo Wilson

Printed in Italy

contents

introduction

Around the world the seas and oceans vary greatly in their character, their climate, and the civilizations they foster along their shores. The nature of the seas shapes the lives of a vast number of the world's inhabitants, even those who live far inland.

The oceans have always attracted people. Some of the earliest civilizations grew up along coasts where the sea offered a plentiful supply of food, easy transport, and a defense against attack. Today many of the world's greatest cities still stand on or near the sea, reflecting their origins as ports, trading centers, or strategic strongpoints. The oceans affect many things about a country, from how wealthy it is to its cuisine and customs, from its weather to its myths.

The different character of the world's oceans affects the daily life of hundreds of millions of people. People in the Caribbean and the Gulf of Mexico, for example, fear hurricanes far more than people on the shores of the Baltic in northern Europe. People living on the coral islands of the Pacific regard the seas in a far different way from those living on the coast of Oregon. Great natural harbors such as San Francisco, New York, and Hong Kong form centers of wealth and population.

The oceans have affected history, too. They dictated which peoples came into contact with each other. Geography and naval power decided whether a people might be conquerors of other lands or defeated by invaders. The political shape of the world today owes much to how different nations have controlled the oceans at different times in the past.

How to use this set

Library of the Oceans has a number of features designed to help you find the information you're looking for quickly and get the most out of the books.

Contents: Page 5 of each volume lists all the subjects covered in the book, as well as every box feature.

Where to find: Near the end of every chapter is a box that tells you where you can find related topics. Use them to read in more detail about different aspects of a subject.

Glossary & Bibliography: At the back of the book is a glossary that explains words often used in the set. A bibliography lists other books you can read about the oceans.

Index: An index that covers the entire set appears in each volume.

the Atlantic

The world's oceans differ vastly, and their characters shape the lives of the people who live on their coasts. The relationship between Europeans and the Mediterranean that cradled their civilization, for example, is far different from that between the islanders of the South Pacific and the ocean that surrounds them. The oceans have played a major role in the history, culture, and everyday lives of the majority of the world's population

The Atlantic

The S-shaped Atlantic is the second largest of the world's oceans and separates North and South America in the west from Europe and Africa in the east. It has two distinct parts: The North Atlantic has a varied coastline of large estuaries, islands, and connecting seas. The margins of the north and central Atlantic have long attracted human settlement and have become highly industrialized.

The South Atlantic coasts of South America and Africa, by contrast, are much smoother and emptier. There are long, featureless stretches of sand, especially in Brazil and West Africa. In South America most people are concentrated near cities. Some still inhabit coastal villages, however, living in traditional ways such as by fishing just offshore.

The midocean ridge, an S-shaped chain of submarine mountains, curves through the middle of the Atlantic Ocean basin.

1

The Atlantic Ocean is the world's second largest body of water. Its shallow continental shelves and marginal seas make it a rich source of minerals and marine life.

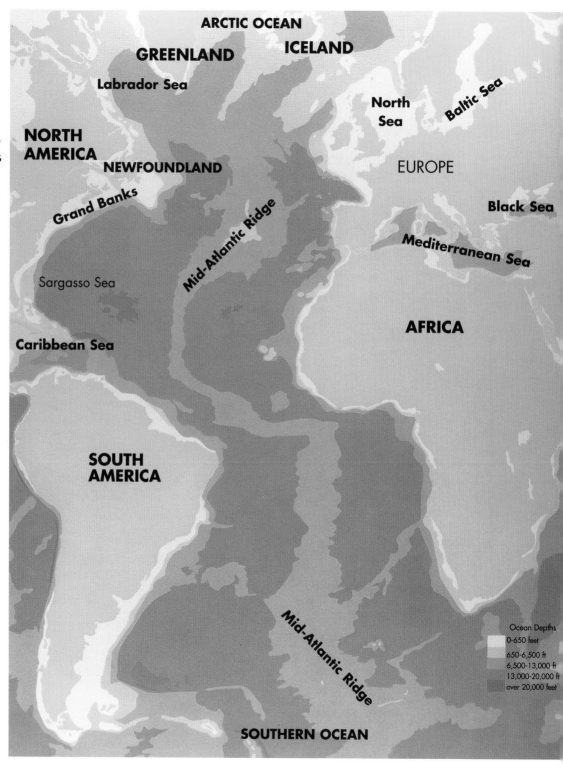

ARCTIC OCEAN

GREENLAND   ICELAND

Labrador Sea

North
Sea   Baltic Sea

NORTH
AMERICA

NEWFOUNDLAND   EUROPE

Grand Banks   Black Sea

Mid-Atlantic Ridge   Mediterranean Sea

Sargasso Sea

AFRICA

Caribbean Sea

SOUTH
AMERICA

Mid-Atlantic Ridge

Ocean Depths
0–650 feet
650–6,500 ft
6,500–13,000 ft
13,000–20,000 ft
over 20,000 feet

SOUTHERN OCEAN

The Sargasso Sea

On his journey across the Atlantic in 1492 Christopher Colombus found clumps of floating grass. He believed this meant that land was nearby. He was wrong. Instead, he had found a sea within the ocean, the Sargasso Sea.

The Sargasso Sea forms an oval between the Bahamas and the Azores. It is a patch of relatively still water held within the North Atlantic Gyre, a vast system of circulating currents.

The "grass" Colombus found was actually sargassum, an alga that only lives here. The weed in turn forms the basis for an entire community of often unique organisms. Some creatures visit this sea: Eels migrate here to spawn before returning to the rivers of Europe and North America.

The living harvest

The Atlantic is rich in fish. The land masses on both sides of the Atlantic slope down toward the ocean, so it receives water from many great rivers. Brazil's Amazon River alone accounts for around a quarter of all the water Earth's oceans receive from rivers. This freshwater is high in nutrients that support the plankton at the base of the marine food chain.

The North Atlantic has been intensively fished for centuries. Fish drew Europeans across the Atlantic as long as 500 years ago, when fishermen seeking new fishing grounds were inspired by a trip made by John Cabot from England to Newfoundland in 1497. The Grand Banks off New England were once one of the richest fisheries in the world. Today, however, the Atlantic is in danger of being

An Inuit boy in northern Canada loads Arctic char into a bag ready to take home. The Inuit depend on the rich life in the northern oceans.

overfished with huge nets that catch young fish before they have chance to breed. One remedy has been to farm fish such as salmon along the coast, particularly in countries such as Scotland and Norway.

The rich life of the North Atlantic depends partly on its waters mixing with those of the Arctic Ocean (*see page 52*). Spring, when the Arctic sea ice melts and releases freshwater into the ocean, brings a bloom of phytoplankton, the microscopic plants that are the basis of life in the ocean. These sustain zooplankton, or animal plankton, and then – directly or indirectly – mollusks, fish, and even great mammals such as baleen whales.

The Baltic and the North Sea

The Baltic and North Sea of northern Europe are very different in character. The Baltic is a narrow sea that cuts the Scandinavian peninsula off from the rest of Europe; the North Sea lies between Europe and the British isles. The Baltic is stagnant, low in salt, and polluted with industrial waste from many rivers. This pollution can cause abnormal amounts of algae. In 1988, for example, algal blooms killed many fish.

The Baltic's poor circulation worsens its problems. Only a small current flows in from the North Sea through the narrow straits of Skagerrak and Kattegat. Once in 20 years or so winds and air pressure strengthen this current and it brings some oxygen-rich water to the Baltic. Although the water of the Baltic is of poor quality, various fish live there, including adapted freshwater species such as bream and perch; herring is the most common saltwater fish.

The Norwegian coast was carved by massive glaciers that left deep flooded valleys called fjords.

Low circulation and a northerly position make the Baltic prone to severe winter storms and freezing. Ice-breakers keep open the major ports such as Copenhagen in Denmark, Helsinki in Finland, and Gdansk in Poland. Such ports are old centers for ship-building, since communication by water has always been important in a region of snow and impassable mountains.

The North Sea, in contrast, never freezes in winter. It is less enclosed, and the Gulf Stream warms it. Its waters are rich fishing grounds, and fishing has long sustained communities on its shores. The North Sea is also rich in mineral resources. Gravel and sand are sucked up from the sea floor, and oil and gas were discovered in 1959.

The galleys of the British king Alfred the Great battle with invading Vikings in the year 897.

Raiders and traders

Seafaring has a long tradition in the Baltic and the North Sea. The Norsemen or Vikings of Norway, for example, traveled overseas to find land to farm between the 8th and 11th centuries. They crossed the rough North Sea and North Atlantic to settle Iceland and Greenland. From here

they probably landed on the east coast of America. From Norway and Denmark they raided and traded throughout Europe to the Mediterranean.

The Baltic and North Sea remained important for trade. Around 1260 a group of German towns joined together in the Hanseatic League to dominate trade in the region. After 1600 the Dutch became a great power thanks to sea trade; they bought what is now New York from the Native Americans and called it New Am-

An oil platform in the North Sea burns off the natural gas that overlays an oil deposit. The oceans' rich mineral resources are a vital source of fossil fuels.

The Gulf Stream

The Gulf Stream forms part of the North Atlantic Gyre, a vast system of circulating sea currents. From the Gulf of Mexico it passes Florida as the warm, swift Florida Current. It is joined by the Antilles Current to flow northeast. East of the Grand Banks of Newfoundland it meets the cold Labrador Current and flows east as the North Atlantic Drift. It then splits. One branch flows south to rejoin the gyre; another continues along the coasts of northwest Europe to the Arctic.

The Gulf Stream is vital in carrying warmth from the Equator to the north, giving northwest Europe its mild climate. Newfoundland, however, is influenced by the cold Labrador Current. Although further south than Britain, it is only frost-free in July.

sterdam. In the 18th century Britain replaced the Dutch as Europe's leading naval power. The British used their command of the seas to create, by the following century, the largest empire the world had ever seen.

The Mediterranean

The Mediterranean and Black seas, which are linked by the narrow Bosporus, are both almost landlocked. The Mediterranean receives surface water from the Atlantic through the Strait of Gibraltar, while deeper water flows out. The rate of circulation is high, so the water in the Mediterranean is completely renewed about every 75 years. The Black Sea, by contrast, receives so little water through the Bosporus that below about 215 ft (65 m) its waters are stagnant.

The Mediterranean has only moderate resources. Its modest fish stocks are overfished. Oil and gas are extracted off the coasts of Italy, Egypt, Algeria, and Libya. The Black Sea attracts people with the supposed healing properties of the mineral springs of its coasts.

The western Mediterranean from space, showing the Strait of Gibraltar (bottom left) through which the sea exchanges water with the Atlantic Ocean.

A vital route

The Mediterranean has always been an important waterway for the exchange of goods, ideas, and people between Asia to the east and Europe to the west. Many civilizations grew along its shores.

The Nile River ends in a delta in the eastern Mediterranean (bottom). The river sustained the civilization of the ancient Egyptians.

Cradle of civilization

Great civilizations clustered around the Mediterranean and sailed its waters as long as 3,500 years ago. The ancient Egyptians and Phoenicians lived here. The Greeks founded cities on the Black Sea, and in France and Italy. Their ideas of medicine, astronomy, and mathematics passed to the Romans, who dominated the Mediterranean basin until the early 5th century. The Arabs took their place, creating an empire that stretched to Spain, Portugal, north Africa, the eastern Mediterranean, and India.

But in 1498 Vasco da Gama discovered a sea route to the East by rounding the Cape of Good Hope at the tip of Africa. The Mediterranean lost its key role as a trade route for some 400 years. Then in 1869 the Suez Canal opened, cutting through Egypt to link the Mediterranean with the Red Sea and the Indian Ocean beyond. The 105-

A wall painting from a tomb in Thebes depicts ancient Egyptian workers loading a cargo ship with wheat. The desire for trade was the driving force for maritime exploration throughout the Old World.

Pirates

In 1523 the French pirate Jean Fleury captured two ships off Cape St. Vincent in Portugal. They were Spanish treasure ships, returning from their new American colonies (*see page 21*) laden with gold dust and ingots, pearls, emeralds, topaz, Aztec masks, and rings. This news of this plunder was electrifying. First France, then England, and later the Dutch sent out privateers, or licensed pirates, to prey on the Spanish in the Caribbean.

The pirates looted, raided, and burned. The Spanish had to defend their ports with heavily manned fortresses and organize their treasure boats into armed fleets.

In 1573 Francis Drake of England teamed up with some Frenchmen and runaway slaves to ambush a treasure-laden caravan in Panama. Drake's personal haul included 15 tons of silver, and back home he became a national hero. Elizabeth I affectionately called him "my pirate."

By the 1620s a group of buccaneers, who became known as the Brethren of the Coast, lived off the coast of Hispaniola. From here they launched their attacks on Spanish galleons returning home. Sometimes they joined forces for a major raid, such as the attack and destruction of Panama City in 1671, led by the famous pirate Henry Morgan. Such ferocious, persistent, and effective attacks weakened Spain's grip on its empire.

Henry Morgan leads the pirate raid on Panama City in 1671.

mile (168-km) canal cut thousands of miles off the sea journey and made the Mediterranean a vital sea route again. Today the huge ships that use it carry oil, gas, and iron ore.

The Caribbean and the Gulf of Mexico

The two westernmost seas of the Atlantic, together called the Central American Sea, are quite distinct. The Caribbean is sheltered from the larger Atlantic by the arc of islands that comprise the West Indies, and is dotted with hundreds more islands. The Gulf, on the other hand, is shallower and has only a few islands, the Florida Keys.

Fishermen land their catch on a beach in the Antilles, West Indies. Fishing in the Caribbean relies on small-scale, local operations rather than commercial fishing.

The beautiful islands of the Caribbean range from the largest, Cuba, to tiny strips of sand. On many islands the tropical climate, clear water, and palm-fringed beaches have made tourism the major industry. Many people also come to dive and explore the region's coral reefs in an underwater environment that has more in common with parts of the Pacific than with the Atlantic. These reefs make it difficult to use commercial fishing methods in the region. Some Caribbean islands actually have to import fish.

The Gulf of Mexico has a 3,000-mile (4,800-km) indented shoreline notable particularly for the great mangrove swamps that line much of the Florida coastline. The

Yachts cruise the Grenadines in the Caribbean Sea, attracted by white beaches and extensive coral reefs.

mighty Mississippi and other rivers discharge freshwater and sediment into the Gulf. The Mississippi Delta carries so much sediment from the land that it is advancing into the ocean at a rate of about 350 ft (105 m) a year. The mixture of fresh and saltwater is nutritious for marine life. The Gulf is sometimes called the Fertile Fish Crescent. It is home to one of the largest shrimp fisheries in the world. Flounder, snapper, mullet, crabs, and oysters also abound. Oysters are so plentiful off Texas that their shells are even used in road building.

Riches and dangers

The Gulf's other great resources are its minerals. People have mined the rich continental shelf for oil and natural gas since the 1930s. The reserves have attracted industrial development to the area. Mineral extraction and its associated businesses bring wealth to cities such as Houston, Texas, and New Orleans, Louisiana. Countries such as Mexico and Guatemala also extract oil from the Gulf. The Caribbean has smaller reserves off Venezuela and Trinidad and Tobago.

Between July and October hurricanes pose a real hazard throughout the Caribbean and the Gulf. They begin in the Atlantic, where northern and southern trade winds meet to create spiraling columns of air that can accelerate to 200 miles an hour (320 km/h). Often these move northwest from the islands north of Tobago into the Gulf. In 1988 Hurricane

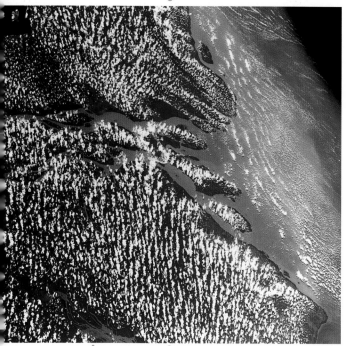

An image from space reveals brown sediment from the Amazon River entering the Atlantic. The mighty river pushes freshwater over 15 miles (24 km) out into the ocean.

Gilbert devastated parts of Jamaica and Mexico. Three months later people in Jamaica still had no fresh food, water, or electricity. The low-lying Florida coast is particularly vulnerable to storms and hurricanes. These can cause tidal surges over 3 feet high (1 m) that flood the islands and miles inland. In 1995 Hurricane Opal struck the Florida coast at 125 miles an hour (200 km/h) and people living in its way were evacuated.

Exploitation and settlement

The peoples of the Atlantic's western and African coasts had existed for thousands of years before Europeans came into contact with them. North America was home to around a million American Indians belonging to various peoples; Central and South America were home to the great civilizations of the Aztecs and Mayas, themselves the heirs

The southern tip of Florida seen from space. The state is low lying, making it particularly vulnerable to the effects of storms and flooding.

of already ancient cultures. The West Indies had been settled by the gentle Arawak people for some 1,500 years and more recently by the Caribs of South America.

The coming of the Europeans devastated these peoples. In 1492 Christopher Columbus landed in the Caribbean while searching for a sea route to the spice islands of Asia. Instead he found supplies of gold that soon brought other Spanish invaders (*see page 18*). Within 14 years of the Spaniards' arrival in 1519 the ancient civilizations of the Mexican Aztecs and the Incas of Peru were destroyed, partly by violence by the Spanish, and partly by the spread of European diseases such as smallpox. The Caribbean islands were likewise depopulated, so that the Spanish had to import slaves from West Africa to farm their sugar plantations.

When North America was settled later the result was equally devastating for the native people. From the early 1600s European settlers forced native Americans off the land. By 1890 those few who survived were forced onto reservations. Not until the 20th century did native Americans gain full rights of citizenship.

A cargo ship is lifted above sea level in a lock chamber as it moves through the Panama Canal. The canal was opened in 1914 to connect the Atlantic and Pacific oceans through the narrowest part of Central America.

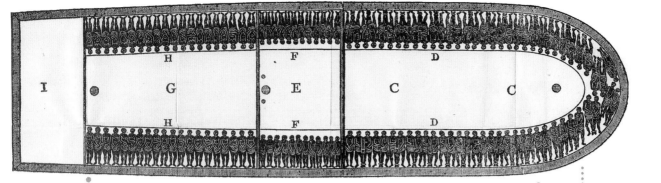

The slave trade

The Spanish in the West Indies used the native people as slaves on their sugar plantations. When brutal treatment all but wiped these people out the Spanish looked elsewhere for slaves. They found them on the Guinea coast of Africa.

Soon a triangular trade developed. Goods were exported from Europe to Africa, from where slaves were transported to the West Indies. Here they were exchanged for goods such as sugar to be sold in Europe. Vast profits were made; ports such as Bristol, London, and Nantes became rich.

The slave trade was finally abolished in 1888, ending centuries of forced immigration. The enslaved people and their descendants have played a huge part in Caribbean and American culture.

The loading plan for slaves on a 19th-century transport ship. By packing the slaves as tightly as possible, the traders could maximize their profits.

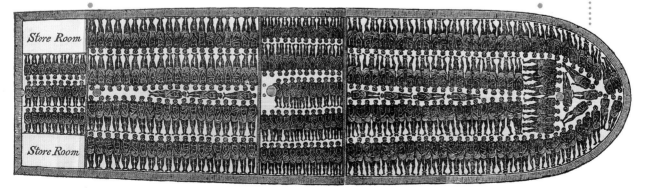

the Pacific

The Pacific is the largest ocean on Earth, occupying one-third of its surface. It contains twice the volume of water of the Atlantic, and its trenches reach the greatest depth of any ocean, the deepest being the Mariana Trench, which is almost 7 miles (11 km) deep.

The Pacific's eastern edge is the relatively smooth seaboard that runs from Alaska to Tierra del Fuego at the tip of South America. The western coast is formed by Russia, China, and southeast Asia. It is far more irregular, with large peninsulas and continental islands such as Indonesia and the Philippines. In the South Pacific lie Australia and New Zealand. The scattered islands of the open seas are known collectively as Oceania. They are divided into three groups: Melanesia, or the "black islands"; Micronesia, the "small islands"; and Polynesia, which means the "many islands."

The largest of these island groups is Polynesia, which is a great triangle with Hawaii at its apex. Its eastern corner falls at lonely Easter Island; the final corner lies at New Zealand 5,000 miles (8,000 km) to the southwest.

Populating the Pacific

Oceania has a long history of settlement. The islands of Melanesia were probably settled some 60,000 years ago by people from southeast Asia. The sea level might have been so low then that they could walk most of the way.

The Pacific Ocean covers more than a third of the globe.

The Pacific Ocean is the largest body of water on the planet. The deep trenches at its edges mark the meeting points of tectonic plates in areas of high geologic activity.

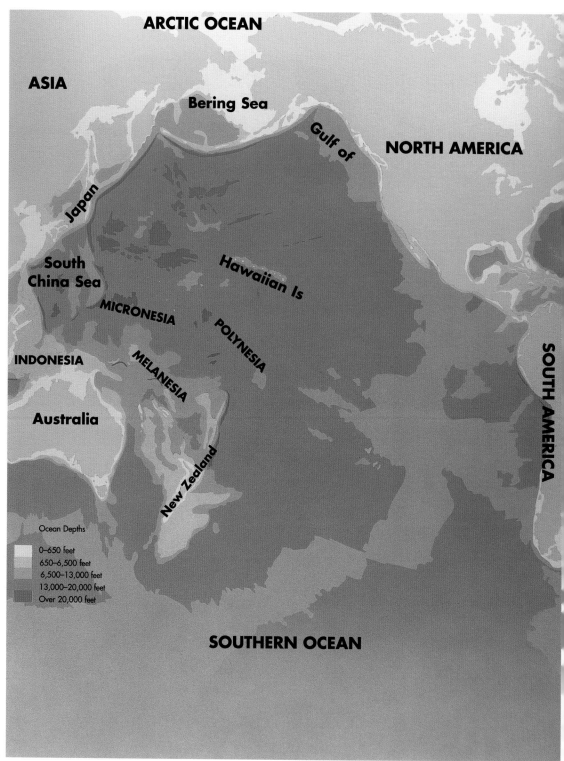

ARCTIC OCEAN

ASIA

Bering Sea

Gulf of

NORTH AMERICA

Japan

Hawaiian Is

South China Sea

MICRONESIA

POLYNESIA

INDONESIA

MELANESIA

Australia

SOUTH AMERICA

New Zealand

Ocean Depths

0–650 feet
650–6,500 feet
6,500–13,000 feet
13,000–20,000 feet
Over 20,000 feet

SOUTHERN OCEAN

Some 3,000 to 4,000 years ago voyagers from Melanesia gradually explored and settled the islands of Micronesia to the north and Polynesia in the east. The last settlement took place some 1,000 years ago when the Maoris, a Polynesian people, arrived on New Zealand.

The peopling of Polynesia involved extraordinary feats of navigation over enormous distances in outrigger canoes. The voyagers had no mechanical aids. Instead, they applied their understanding of wind and weather patterns, cloud formations, bird behavior, sea color as an indicator of ocean or coastal currents, and the positions of the sun, moon, and stars.

Easter Island, the easternmost inhabited island of Polynesia, is typical of the waves of settlement that have occurred in the Pacific. An ancient people once lived on this remote island and created the huge statues in volcanic stone, up to 37 ft (11 m) tall, for which it is known. In about 1700 Polynesian settlers occupied the islands; they in turn were nearly wiped out by slavery and smallpox in the 1860s after being discovered by Europeans.

The Moai statues on Easter Island were carved by an ancient seafaring people.

Colonization
The Portuguese explorer Ferdinand Magellan was the first

The British navigator
Captain James Cook claims New South Wales, Australia, for Britain in 1770.

European to negotiate a sea route to the East across the Pacific via the tip of South America. The system of channels between the tip of the continent and Tierra del Fuego, now called the Strait of Magellan, were hard to navigate, and Magellan had a rough passage. When he and his crew at last reached the calm ocean, he named it the Pacific, which means peaceful.

European explorers discovered the Pacific islands long after the Atlantic shores of North and South America had been mapped. Although Magellan visited the Mariana Islands in 1520, other areas remained uncharted until 1800. In three voyages toward the end of the 18th century, the British captain James Cook charted New Zealand and New

South Wales, Antarctica, the New Hebrides, New Caledonia, Hawaii, and the Pacific coast of North America.

European domination

The Europeans dominated the region for 200 years, using the islands as sources of coconut oil, sandalwood, pineapple, coffee, and sugarcane. The British established penal colonies in Australia. By the 1960s, when many Pacific nations won their independence, the original island people were outnumbered by immigrants on islands such as Hawaii, New Zealand, Fiji, and Australia. Hawaii became the 50th U.S. state in 1959. New Zealand and Australia, once British colonies, are now sovereign nations.

The South China Sea

The South China Sea is the largest marginal sea of the Pacific. Today it forms an important shipping route to the Indian Ocean, bordering the densely populated area of

Cultured half-pearls in an oyster from Thailand. A cultured pearl is one that forms around grit that has been deliberately placed in the oyster.

The ruins of the Port Arthur penal settlement in Australia. British criminals shipped here during the 19th century suffered from harsh and cruel conditions.

A traditional Chinese junk sails into a very modern Hong Kong harbor. The close proximity of the old ways and new technology is typical of large Asian cities.

southeast Asia. The sea contains plenty of fish, almost all consumed locally.

For a long time the emperors of China allowed only one port, Canton (now Guangzhou), to trade with foreigners, since they felt that China should be self-sufficient. In the 10th century, however, the Sung empire came under attack, so ports were opened up, and boats equipped for war.

Seaborne trade increased as the overland route to China was disrupted by the hostile Mongol peoples. Arab merchants sailed to south China to buy silk, porcelain, and tea. These filtered through to Europe, along with the Chinese inventions of gunpowder, paper, and printing.

The Ming dynasty, which came to power in 1368, once again outlawed foreign trade, but outside forces could not be kept out once the Europeans discovered the sea route to the spice islands. Merchants came in great numbers. The

Portuguese, the Dutch, and the English all gradually resumed trading in Canton and Shanghai.

Pacific trade

Some of the world's fastest-growing economies today lie in the western Pacific. They are all based on high-value manufactured goods. Japan set the pace, followed by Taiwan, South Korea, Indonesia, and Malaysia.

Today Japan is the biggest trading nation on the Pacific, with the exception of the United States. Japanese exports include cars and electronic goods. Taiwan, meanwhile, made its name with aircraft parts and computers. In return

The people of the Solomon Islands in the western Pacific have created an artificial island by building their houses on stilts. Island people have an intimate relationship with the sea, relying on it for almost all of their material needs.

Pirates of the Pacific

In the early 19th century the South China Sea was dominated by huge, disciplined fleets of pirates, led by Ching Yih. Men, women, and children lived permanently on the ships, as if in villages. In much the same way the coastal people had always lived on boats around the ports and rivers of southern China.

The pirates numbered about 50,000 and plundered local fishing craft and foreign merchant vessels alike. Chin Yih died in 1807, after which his wife Ching Shih took over. Her fleet fought off all government attempts to destroy it, until she finally secured an amnesty, or official pardon, for herself and her pirates. She later ran a gambling house in Canton.

A container terminal at the major Japanese city and port of Kobe. Japan's expertise in ocean trade has contributed to its current economic strength.

these countries import materials such as petroleum from the Persian Gulf, coal from India, and grain from North America. Two-fifths of all the United States' trade is with Pacific nations such as Japan, Hong Kong, Singapore, Thailand, and Malaysia.

During the 1980s even China, which was for a long time closed to the west, began operating an "open-door" policy to encourage foreign trade. On the coast the Chinese have created Special Economic Zones where foreign companies are encouraged to operate businesses in association with the Chinese. New ports have been built to serve these areas, such as at Shenzen, near Hong Kong, and on the island of Xiamen, which trades with Taiwan and southeast Asian ports.

Trade routes

The Pacific is crossed by some of the world's most important trade routes. The geography of the ocean's shores encourages sea trade. The Asian coasts and islands are heavily indented with natural harbors. The West Coast of the United States, despite the inhospitality of the rugged coast of the Pacific Northwest or around Big Sur in California, offers good ports at Los Angeles, San Diego, and San Francisco. San Francisco Bay is one of the world's greatest natural harbors.

The "Ring of Fire"

The Pacific is home to some of the world's most active geo-logic hot spots. There are so many volcanoes on the groups of islands around the ocean's edge, the Pacific Rim, that they are known collectively as the "Ring of Fire." The geological activity, which is concentrated where the plates of the earth's crust meet, also creates earthquake zones. In 1995 an earthquake in the city of Kobe, in Japan, for example, killed 5,400 people. The shores of the Pacific are also prone to the effect of tsunamis, giant waves created by undersea earthquakes or volcanoes. These waves travel miles across the open ocean and inundate the coastlines.

Coral reefs

Although the islands of the Ring of Fire are volcanic, many Pacific islands are coral atolls (*see page 47*). They are made up of the skeletons of millions of tiny creatures called polyps, which accumulate at the rate of about 6 inches (15 cm) a year.

Coral reefs are rich habitats, with caves, tunnels, ridges, and pinnacles that provide protection and food for colorful fish species, as well as turtles, giant clams, anemones, starfish, urchins, shrimps, and lobsters. The Pacific is home to the world's largest coral reef, the Great Barrier Reef off northeast Australia. It is over 1,250 miles (2,000 km) long and some 90 miles (150 km) broad at its widest.

Big Sur in California has a grandeur and serenity that typifies for many people this popular part of the Pacific.

The reef's ecosystem

Coral reefs are complex ecosystems. Their best guardians are probably the islanders who have known them longest. In the Yap Islands, for example, people fish from outrigger canoes or dive down to impale reef creatures with bamboo harpoons, using torches to attract fish at night. They make tools from the coral and medicines from its toxins, but they also understand the need to preserve the reef's resources. Some islands have strict rules. On Papua New Guinea, for example, it is forbidden to catch small fish. In Fiji turtle-hunting is banned during the animal's spawning season.

The greatest concentration of coral reefs is found in the Pacific Ocean. The vast number of small oceanic islands, combined with the warm, clear waters, allows reef communities to flourish.

Nuclear Testing

The coral atolls also have more sinister uses. Since World War II ended in 1945, countries in Europe and America have taken advantage of the isolation of the Pacific islands to use the region as a test ground for nuclear weapons. From 1946 to 1962 the United States used Bikini and Eniwetok atolls in the Marshall Islands as

The Asmat people of Indonesia perform ceremonies to worship the gods that live in the sea.

bases to test nuclear and hydrogen bombs. As recently as 1995 the French government defied public opinion at home and in the Pacific to test a number of nuclear devices on Mururoa in French Polynesia.

Fishing

Although the Pacific is extremely rich in fish, the countries that border it are densely populated. It is therefore a heavily fished ocean, yielding three-fifths of the global catch, mainly from coastal waters. Where fish occur, they occur in abundance, and often in a variety of species. There are, for example, six types of tuna, while anchovy, sardine, salmon, and shellfish are much sought after.

Bora Bora in French Polynesia is an island slowly evolving into a coral atoll. Its extinct volcano is gradually sinking, and once the inner island disappears, a true atoll will be formed.

On the Yangtze Delta

China's largest river, the Yangtze, meets the East China Sea in a massive complex of waterways, canals, and low-lying land. A system of dikes and sluices on the seaward side protects the land, and the dikes have been extended to reclaim land for farming. Water levels are controlled, and crops are planned and managed carefully.

Cotton, rice, corn, sugarcane, and fruit grow alongside ponds where fish are cultivated. In a self-sustaining cycle sheep are raised on a diet of mulberry leaves. The leaves of the trees feed silkworms. Sheep and silkworms also fertilize the pond mud, which is then removed to enrich the rice fields.

China, Japan, Russia, the United States, Peru, Chile, South Korea, and Indonesia are all major fishing nations. Fish are an essential source of protein in Pacific countries and a staple of Oriental food.

The fishing fortunes of countries rise and fall with fish numbers. Peru, for example, has slipped from its position as world leader in 1970 because of changes to the local anchovy population. The Peruvian anchovy catch once made up a remarkable 20% of the global fish catch. But due to overfishing and to irregular weather patterns known as El Niño, their numbers declined, the fishery collapsed, and local people lost their livelihood (*see page 39*).

To overcome the problem, some countries raise fish in pens in coastal waters. Japan is a world leader in this, farming shrimps, mussels, oysters, and tuna. Hong Kong, which is one of the world's most densely populated cities, relies on vast islands of floating pens to raise its seafood.

A vanishing way of life

Although some island peoples still live as their ancestors did, preferring traditional fishing methods to commercial techniques, for example, most have adopted Western ways. Many of the smaller islands receive financial aid from various international agencies. This has sometimes meant the introduction of a Western-style disposable culture instead of self-sustaining practices. Drinking water may be imported in bottles and fish in cans. Some communities have sold fishing rights, which means there are fewer stocks for local fishermen. In some areas people are protesting the changes. In French Polynesia, for example, the people are demanding more autonomy, with a return to traditional ways of trading.

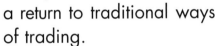

Winds and currents

The serenely named Pacific Ocean is notorious for its typhoons, or hurricanes. These occur mainly east of the Philippines and in the South and East China seas. They begin in low-pressure regions, attracting winds

An Indonesian fisherman uses a traditional net to catch milkfish. Artisanal fishing methods remain an important way of obtaining food in the developing nations of Southeast Asia.

Artisanal fishermen in Brunei remove the valuable skin from a large estuarine crocodile.

Marine iguanas sun themselves on an island of the Galápagos. The long-term isolation of Pacific islands has given rise to many unique species of plants and animals.

that rush in to fill the low pressure, causing air to spiral with increasing fury into a hurricane.

The circular surface currents, or gyres, of the Pacific are driven by easterly winds just on either side of the equator and by westerly winds further to the north and south. The clockwise North Pacific Gyre includes the westward flowing North Equatorial Current, which is diverted north at the Philippines to form the Japan Current. This brings warmth to Japan.

Running east as the North Pacific Drift, the current is joined by the cold Oyashio, or "Mother Current," from the Bering Sea. Together they flow down the west coast of North America. A branch of the North Pacific Drift reaches Alaska, where it keeps the south coast ice-free in winter but causes frequent rain.

In the South Pacific, meanwhile, the gyre runs counterclockwise. Its eastern section, the Peru Current, flows up the west coast of South America. Cold southerly winds blowing along it create coastal deserts in northern Chile and Peru. Every few years the current is disrupted by the El Niño effect.

The Bering Sea

The Bering Sea is the most northern sea of the Pacific, separating Asia from North America. It leads via the narrow Bering Strait into the Arctic Ocean (*see page 52*).

About 20,000 years ago the sea level in the strait dropped so that for several centuries it became a land bridge from Asia to what is now Alaska. It was across this bridge that early humans crossed to settle the uninhabited American continent.

The Bering Sea is difficult to navigate, with cold temperatures, icebergs, and many violent storms. Nevertheless, it is an important sea route for Russia to the port of Arkhangel'sk, which lies in the extreme northwest of the country.

Hurricane waves lash the harbor of a Samoan city. Rising warm air from the equatorial Pacific causes violent storms throughout the region.

El Niño

Every few years the Pacific coastal waters off Peru suffer an abnormal change in current and wind patterns that kills much of the local marine life, particularly the commercially important anchovies. The phenomenon is called El Niño, "the child," for the Christ child, because it often occurs around Christmas. The southerly winds drop, allowing warm water to run down from the equator and displace the cold, nutrient-rich Peru Current. The warm water has less oxygen and nutrients, so plankton and fish die in huge numbers, bringing devastation to local fishermen.

the Indian Ocean & Arabian Sea

The Indian Ocean and the associated Arabian Sea are the third largest of the world's oceans. They differ from the Pacific and the Atlantic in several ways, particularly in that they are more enclosed. Continental Asia prevents their waters having any contact with cold water from the Arctic in the far north; they are isolated by Africa from the Atlantic in the west and mix only slightly with the Pacific around the island groups of southeast Asia. They have less variation in their climate than the other oceans, being mainly tropical and temperate.

But this more stable climate does not mean that the region is not biologically rich. The Indian Ocean is home to shallows that sustain the highest diversity of marine species in the world. They lie in the so-called Indo-West Pacific, between the Indian Ocean and the Pacific, where creatures from both oceans congregate. The warm, shallow waters of the Persian Gulf, meanwhile, support extensive coral reefs.

Coastline

The coasts of the Indian Ocean are very varied, ranging from enormous deltas to estuaries, marshes, swamps, coral reefs, cliffs, and beaches. The Sundarbans, on the Ganges-Brahmaputra Delta of the Indian subcontinent, are home to the largest mangrove swamps in the world.

The shape of the Indian Ocean and the Arabian Sea.

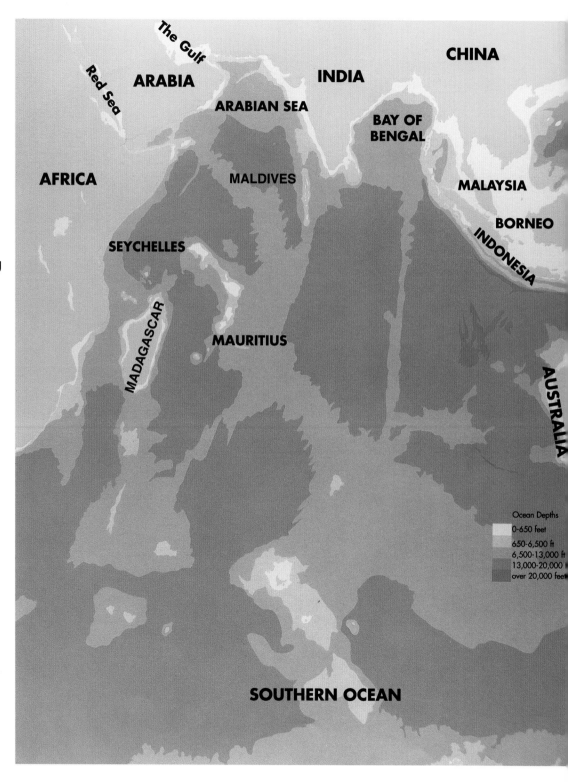

The Indian Ocean is a comparatively young ocean, being only 170 million years old. It is still spreading along the ridge that runs out of the Red Sea into the Arabian Sea.

The Gulf

Red Sea

ARABIA

INDIA

CHINA

ARABIAN SEA

BAY OF BENGAL

AFRICA

MALDIVES

MALAYSIA

BORNEO

INDONESIA

SEYCHELLES

MADAGASCAR

MAURITIUS

AUSTRALIA

Ocean Depths
0-650 feet
650-6,500 ft
6,500-13,000 ft
13,000-20,000 ft
over 20,000 feet

SOUTHERN OCEAN

The Indian Ocean receives more river sediment than all the other oceans put together. Large rivers, such as the Ganges, carry vast amounts of eroded soil and rock from the Himalaya mountains. The sediment settles in great fans from the river mouths, affecting the shape of the continental shelf. The water is less than 600 feet (185 m) deep for 100 miles (160 km) out to sea, where the fans run out and the depth suddenly doubles.

A mouth of the Ganges-Brahmaputra Delta in India washes vast amounts of sediment (*light blue*) into the ocean.

Currents and monsoons

The Indian Ocean's greatest interchange of water is in the south with the Southern Ocean of Antarctica. The deep-lying, cold polar water moves north only sluggishly. At the surface, however, circulation is vigorous, powered by the seasonal winds known as monsoons.

Between November and April the northeast monsoon creates a counterclockwise gyre in the Arabian Sea and a clockwise one in the Bay of Bengal. Around the equator the North Equatorial Current flows west. Between May and October, however, the winds change direction. The southwest monsoon reverses the gyres in the Arabian Sea and the Bay of Bengal, while the North Equatorial Current flows east and is known as the Monsoon Current. In the southern Indian Ocean the gyre remains constant, always flowing counterclockwise.

Stilt fishermen fish off the coast of Sri Lanka. The stilts enable them to fish in deeper water without having to build boats.

The southwest monsoon wind picks up vast amounts of moisture as it travels over the ocean, bringing torrential rain to southern Asia. In spring and fall, before and after these rains, cyclones occur over the ocean. These hurricane-force storms bring havoc to low-lying coastal areas such as Bangladesh, one of the most densely populated regions in the world.

Fishing

The warm Indian Ocean has fewer fish than the Atlantic or Pacific. In some areas, however, such as the northern Arabian Sea and on the south African coast, upwelling occurs during the southwest monsoon, and cold, nutrient-rich water is drawn to the surface. Here many fish, such as shrimp, snapper, skate, and anchovy, can thrive.

Buddhism by sea

The oceans have played an important part in the spread of some of the world's major religions, including Islam and Christianity. The spread of Buddhism from India throughout Southeast Asia is another example. The third-century B.C. emperor Asoka of India sent missionaries by ship to the island of Sri Lanka to convert people there.

Buddhism spread elsewhere among the islands and coastal regions of Southeast Asia. The religion's missionaries sailed with the traders on well-established trade routes that linked places such as the islands of Indonesia with such distant destinations as ancient Rome, in Europe.

These villagers in Bangladesh lose their homes each time floods wash away part of their land. A 3-foot (1-m) rise in sea level would make 12 million Bangladeshis homeless.

Local fishing is often small-scale but provides an essential food for coastal people. The old methods are still used, and in Sri Lanka, for example, the fishermen sit on tall wooden stilts to fish in deep water.

Tuna is widely fished out at sea, particularly in the western Indian Ocean, and attracts the major fishing countries, such as Japan, Russia, and Taiwan.

Early trade

The monsoons can be a blessing as well as a curse. They bring devastating

floods, yet it was sailors' mastery of the regular winds and predictable currents that encouraged the early development of the region's trade. The Arabs were the ocean's great traders, establishing ports along the east coast of Africa and around the coast of India. The Arab influence is still evident around the ocean. The Swahili language of the east coast of Africa is an Arab dialect, for example, and many people there follow the Arabs' Muslim religion. Later the Buddhist religion, which originated in India, spread to Southeast Asia by sea.

The Arabs' trading network was well established by the time the first Europeans arrived. The Portuguese explorer Vasco da Gama crossed the Indian Ocean in 1498. His masters were determined to trade with the wealthy rulers of India. After a series of battles against the Arabs the Europeans came to dominate the region, establishing trading posts in Goa, Calicut, and Cochin on the east coast of India.

Unique islands
The Indian Ocean is home to many islands. The largest is Madagascar, which broke off from the continental mainland when Africa and India split

The dodo used to live on the island of Mauritius but became extinct between 1665 and 1670, after Europeans arrived.

46

between 160 and 45 million years ago. The island has been isolated for so long that some animals only occur there. They include 40 types of lemur, a long-tailed, tree-living mammal related to the monkey. The volcanic island of Mauritius, meanwhile, was the only home of the dodo. This flightless bird was hunted to extinction by European settlers in the 17th century.

Many of the ocean's island groups are coral atolls. These atolls are created when coral forms around a volcanic island that then sinks, leaving a broken coral reef around a lagoon. In the Indian Ocean these atolls sometimes contain smaller reefs with inner islands and lagoons. Such atolls-within-atolls are typical of the Maldive Islands,

Statues of Buddha in Sri Lanka, where nearly three-quarters of the population are Buddhists. Buddhism spread through Southeast Asia by sea.

which number about 1,000. The Seychelles, on the other hand, combine low coral islands with high continental ones covered in lush vegetation. Both island groups attract tourists, but the reef environment is threatened by the harvesting of coral, and the demands of tourism can undermine fragile island environments.

Oil fires burned in Kuwait for weeks after the end of the Gulf War in 1991, bringing devastating pollution to the coasts of Kuwait and Saudi Arabia.

The Arabian and Red seas

The Arabian Sea is the name given to the part of the Indian Ocean that lies between Arabia and India. At the Arabian peninsula it splits into two long arms, the Red Sea to the west and the Persian or Arabian Gulf to the east. The Gulf was the focus of the short-lived Gulf War of 1991, when an Allied coalition defeated Iraq. Despite its lack of freshwater and fertile soil, the region has long attracted international interest because it is rich in minerals, particularly oil (*see page 51*).

The Red Sea, despite its name, is blue, though it is sometimes tinged reddish-brown by algae. It is separated by a narrow strait from the Arabian Sea, so there is little interchange of water between them. Its high evaporation rate makes its waters hot and salty. The conditions have encouraged the creation of extensive coral reefs.

The Red Sea is one of the world's youngest seas. In contrast with the 200-million-year-old Atlantic, for example, it is only about 20 million years old, having been formed when the continents of Asia and Africa separated. This created a rift valley that filled with water and widened to form a narrow sea. Geologists believe that the Red Sea will widen as the Arabian Peninsula and Africa move apart until it one day forms an open ocean between them.

Early civilizations

The Gulf and the Red Sea helped support some of the earliest recorded civilizations. The Sumerians, for example, lived in cities between the Tigris and Euphrates rivers at the head of the Gulf from around 3500 B.C. A thousand years later the ancient Egyptians traded across the Red Sea with a land they called Punt. They built a canal between the Nile River and the Red Sea, and used the sea

A space image of the Red Sea (*left*) shows how the sea splits into two thin arms at its head, the Gulf of Suez and the Gulf of Aqaba. The thin blue line that connects the Gulf of Suez with the Mediterranean (*right*) is the Suez Canal, built to shorten the sea journey from Europe to Asia.

Traditional fishing nets on the Arabian Sea. Fish such as shrimp, snapper, sardine, and anchovy thrive where upwelling occurs during the monsoon season.

as a springboard for finding a sea route to India. In about 146 B.C. a sailor called Eudoxus reached India and returned with precious stones and spices.

Rich resources

In contrast to the infertile, desert land that often lines their shores, these seas are rich in resources. The Red Sea, in particular, is rich in marine life, mainly thanks to the extensive coral reefs along its shores (*see page 33*). More than 350 species of fish have been recorded here. Snappers, groupers, and parrot fish are caught for local needs, and there is a sardine fishery in the Gulf of Suez. Bahrain, off the coast of Saudi Arabia, is noted for pearl fishers who hold their breath for remarkable lengths of time as they dive to the seabed to pick up oysters.

The low coastal population of the Red Sea means that its coral reefs have been able to develop with little interference from people. Today, however, they are a popular attraction for divers. The increase in human activity has brought a

Dhows, traditional sailing ships, are still made by hand. They are used all along the coast of the Arabian Sea.

very real danger of damage to these fragile environments.

The Gulf and oil

Tourism is not the main threat to the seas, however. Since 1908, when oil was discovered in Iran, the Arabian Gulf has become the biggest oil-producing region in the world. This has brought great wealth to the area, and great problems for the Gulf itself.

The distinctive, steeply angled sail of a traditional dhow is a striking sight off a port on the Arabian Sea.

One threat is from increased shipping. Most of the crude oil is exported in tankers from terminals in Kuwait, Dhahran, and Bahrain to the Far East, Europe, and America. These large ships can be difficult to navigate, especially through the narrow strait that leads out into the Arabian Sea. Accidents often cause oil spills. Probably the single largest spill came not from shipping, however, but from war. The Gulf War of 1991 saw oil wells set alight and a huge oil spill enter the sea. It badly contaminated the coasts of Saudi Arabia and Kuwait, destroying the feeding grounds of about 100,000 wading birds and disrupting the shrimp-fishing season.

Increased human activity of all kinds threatens the Red Sea and the Gulf. For centuries the people on their coasts lived in harmony with them, fishing from wooden boats or sailing to trade with the outside world. Such harmony has to be recaptured before irreparable damage is done.

where to find...

Water in motion **2:**8

Winds and storms **2:**48

Coral reefs **7:**8

Mangroves **7:**28

Great voyages **9:**28

The sea's riches **12:**8

Dirty sea **12:**34

the polar oceans

4

The Arctic Ocean in the north and the Southern or Antarctic Ocean in the south are the earth's two polar oceans. Although they are at the opposite ends of the earth, they are both equally far from the equator, so they have some characteristics in common. In particular they are characterized by extreme cold, by sea ice, and by only minimal human exploitation. There are also many differences between them, however. Whereas the Arctic Ocean is almost enclosed by land, the Southern Ocean mixes freely with the Atlantic and Pacific oceans.

The Arctic Ocean

The world's smallest ocean, the Arctic Ocean is almost enclosed by Canada, Alaska, Russia, Norway, and Greenland. Its most important connection is with the Atlantic, where it exchanges waters via a channel between Greenland and the island of Svalbard. Warmer surface water flows in from the Atlantic as a cold, deep-lying mass exits from the Arctic. This exchange is vital to the circulation and temperature of the North Atlantic Ocean, which in turn affects the temperature of other oceans. The deepest layer

The Arctic
(*top*) is an ocean surrounded by continents, while the Antarctic (*bottom*) is a continent surrounded by ocean.

Antarctica is home to only a handful of research stations belonging to a dozen or so countries.

of water in the Arctic Ocean, Arctic Bottom Water, remains trapped in the basin. It can be as cold as −29.5°F (−1.4°C).

The Southern Ocean

The enormous mass of water that is the Southern Ocean, in contrast, releases great quantities of cold, nutrient-rich water into the Atlantic, Pacific, and Indian oceans without any interference from land. Its main current, the Antarctic Circumpolar Current, or West Wind Drift, is the world's largest and fastest-moving mass of water. It makes a constant clockwise 15,000-mile (24,000-km) circuit of the earth.

The Southern Ocean accounts for over 20 percent of the oceans' surface area but only 10 percent of all oceanic heat. It therefore absorbs a lot of heat, mostly from the Atlantic, which it transfers to the atmosphere, warming the climate of the southern hemisphere.

Ice and icebergs

Both polar oceans can be extremely cold. In winter ice covers around half of the Arctic Ocean. Because it reflects sunlight and prevents waters mixing, it is the main factor in maintaining the

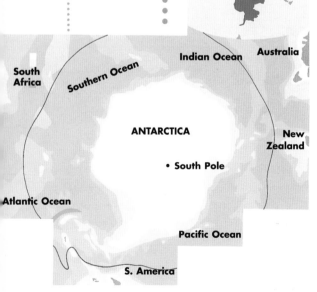

The Arctic Ocean is almost entirely closed in by the European, Asian, and American continents.

ocean's low temperature. The enormous variation in the extent of ice cover affects air and sea temperatures, winds, and currents. Antarctica, meanwhile, contains over 90 percent of the world's ice. Floating shelves of ice border the continent.

In summer the Arctic sea ice reduces to half its winter extent. Great floating icebergs form. They are not chunks of sea ice but have broken off slow-moving rivers of ice called glaciers. When a glacier reaches the sea, it breaks off into icebergs, a process called calving. Thousands of icebergs are formed each year on the west coast of Greenland. Some are eventually carried into the Atlantic. They can weigh as much as 1.5 million tons and stand 260 ft (80 m) out of the water. In the Southern Ocean, meanwhile, the calving season begins in October, at the start of the southern spring.

There are many names for icebergs. Spikey ones are called "pinnacle bergs"; smaller ones "bergy bits"; and ones that make a noise as they melt are "growlers." Unlike Arctic icebergs, those in the Antarctic are flat and regular in shape. Icebergs are about four-fifths submerged, making them dangerous to shipping.

Exploration

Both the Arctic and the Antarctic are inhospitable to humans. While there have long been settle-

Abandoned Inuit turf houses are reclaimed by the dwarfed vegetation of the Arctic tundra, west Greenland.

The splintered remains of a hut are a grim reminder of Sir Robert Falcon Scott's ill-fated race to the South pole. He and four teammates died during the return journey in 1912.

A shrimp-packing factory dominates Jackobshavn harbor in Greenland. Fishing is the island's main industry, providing its chief export as well as food for domestic consumption.

ments around the edges of the Arctic Ocean, the southern continent remains home only to research stations.

The Vikings of Norway first reached the Arctic in about 860 (*see page 14*). Much later, explorers from Europe were inspired by a desire to find a northern passage to East Asia from the Atlantic. The Northeast Passage was navigated by a Swedish baron, A. E. Nordenskiöld, in 1878 and 1879. Today the passage to Vladivostock on Russia's Pacific coast is used regularly and kept open by ice-breakers.

In 1906 the Norwegian Roald Amundsen became the first person to navigate the Northwest Passage. Today its western end is used to supply the Canadian and Alaskan oilfields. In 1911 Amundsen became the first person to reach the South Pole. The British explorer Robert Falcon Scott repeated the feat a month later. He and the other members of his expedition died on their return journey.

People and resources

Despite freezing, inhospitable conditions, people have lived around the Arctic Ocean for thousands of years. The shore-dwellers of the western Arctic are the Inuit, and those of the Aleutian Islands, the Aleut. They live by hunting and fishing. Many of the people in the north of Russia, Finland,

Sweden, and Norway are nomadic Lapps, or Saami, who live by herding reindeer.

Fisheries abound where warmer Atlantic water mixes with the Arctic. The catch includes cod, plaice, and halibut, although stocks are badly reduced due to overfishing. The Southern

Ocean, too, is rich in life. In summer, as melting ice forms a surface layer of freshwater, shrimplike krill swarm in masses over hundreds of square miles, attracting penguins and baleen whales that feast on them.

Development and protection

The discovery of oil on the coast of Alaska in 1968 led to the laying of the trans-Arctic pipeline, which carries crude oil south for export. Further development will be difficult, however, due to the icy conditions.

The Antarctic, meanwhile, belongs to no one. In 1959 it became an area of scientific research under a treaty signed by 12 states, which has since been expanded. The treaty covers such factors as the exchange of information, safety, and the conservation of marine species.

The red huts of a Chilean research station contrast with the bleak Antarctic landscape. The continent remains the world's last great wilderness area.

A Russian fishes through an ice-hole in the Arctic.

glossary

abyss:
the deepest part of the ocean.

archipelago:
a group or chain of islands.

atoll:
a coral island in which a thin reef surrounds a lagoon.

benthic:
a word meaning occurring at the bottom of the sea.

consumers:
the creatures at the higher levels of the food chain who eat either producers or other consumers such as smaller creatures.

continental shelf:
a submerged edge of a continent that forms a shallow part of the seabed, usually no deeper than 660 feet (200 m).

crustaceans:
a class of hard-bodied animals that includes lobsters, shrimps, and crabs.

ecosystem:
the relationship between a community of plants and animals and its environment.

food chain:
an arrangement that divides the animals and plants in a particular environment into levels to show what eats what. Members of each level generally eat members of the level immediately below them and are themselves eaten by members of the next higher level. Food chains are often combined in more complex food webs.

gyre:
a giant circular current on the surface of the ocean.

hot spot:
a source of geologic activity in the earth's mantle that gives rise to volcanoes.

hydrothermal vent:
a superheated spring at the bottom of the ocean.

lagoon:
a shallow lake usually partly separated from the ocean by an obstacle such as a reef or a barrier island.

magma:
molten rock from the earth's mantle.

midocean ridges:
long mountain ranges found in all the world's oceans that are the center of seafloor spreading.

mollusks:
a group of invertebrates that includes most shellfish, snails, clams, and squid.

ooze:
a seafloor sediment formed largely from the shells of dead microorganisms.

pelagic:
a word meaning belonging to the open ocean.

photosynthesis:
the process by which plants convert sunlight and chemicals into foods such as carbohydrates.

plankton:
microscopic organisms that occur in huge numbers in the oceans. Phytoplankton are plants; zooplankton are animals.

producers:
the plants that form the bottom layer of the food chain.

sediment:
fine material such as dust that is deposited by winds, glaciers, and rivers and settles on the ocean bed.

subduction zone:
the area where one of earth's plates is destroyed by sliding beneath the edge of another, creating a trench.

tectonics:
the study of the earth's plates and other large features.

tides:
the periodic rise and fall of the oceans due to the gravity of the moon and the sun.

trench:
a long chasm in the seabed where one of earth's plates slides beneath another. Trenches are the deepest part of the ocean.

tsunami:
a giant wave produced by an underwater earthquake or volcanic eruption.

upwelling:
the process by which cold, often nutrient-rich waters from the deeper ocean rise to the surface, especially near coasts.

bibliography

Blair, Carvel, *Exploring the Sea: Oceanography Today*. Random House, 1986.

Clifford, Nick, *Incredible Earth*. Dorling Kindersley, 1996.

Duxbury, Alyn C. & Alison, *Introduction to the World's Oceans*. William C. Brown Publishing, 1994.

Embry, Lynn, *Scientific Encounters of the Mysterious Sea*. Good Apple, 1988.

Fine, J. C., *Oceans in Peril*. Atheneum, 1987.

Fine, J. C., *Creatures of the Sea*. Atheneum, 1989.

Hendrickson, Robert, *The Ocean Almanac*. Dolphin Books, 1984.

Ingmanson, Dale E., & William J. Wallace, *Oceanography: an Introduction*. 5th edition. Wadsworth, 1995.

Kemp, Peter (ed.), *The Oxford Companion to Ships and the Sea*. Oxford University Press, 1994.

Lambert, David, *The Kingfisher Young People's Book of the Oceans*. Kingfisher Books, 1997.

Lambert, David, & Anita McConnell, *Seas and Oceans*. Facts on File, 1985.

Pernetta, John, *Atlas of the Oceans*. Rand McNally & Co., 1994.

Pinet, Paul R., *Oceanography: An Introduction to the Planet Oceanus*. West Publishing Company, 1992.

Ray, Carleton, *Wildlife of the Polar Regions*. Harry N. Abrams Inc., 1981.

Robinson, W. W., *Incredible Facts about the Ocean: the Land Below, the Life Within*. Silver Burdett Press, 1987.

Robinson, W. W., *Incredible Facts about the Ocean: How We Use It, How We Abuse It*. Dillon Press, 1990.

Simon, Seymour, *How to Be an Ocean Scientist in Your Own Home*. Lippincott-Raven Publishers, 1988.

Stevenson, Robert E., and Frank H. Talbot, *The Illustrated Library of the Earth: Oceans*. Rodale Press, 1994.

picture credits

The sources for the illustrations that appear in this book are listed below. Credits from left to right are separated by semi-colons; top to bottom they are separated by dashes.

9: NOAA. **10:** MC Picture Library. **12, 13:** Planet Earth Pictures; Zefa-Damm. **14, 15:** Mary Evans Picture Library; Richard Folwell/Science Photo Library. **16, 17:** NASA; Planet Earth Pictures; AKG London. **18, 19:** Mary Evans Picture Library; Hutchison Library – Planet Earth Pictures. **21, 21:** NASA (2). **22, 23:** Hutchison Library; Mary Evans Picture Library (2). **25:** NOAA. **26, 27:** MC Picture Library; Planet Earth Pictures. **28, 29:** Mary Evans Picture Library; Hutchison Library – Gina Green. **30, 31:** Hutchison Library (2). **32, 33:** Hutchison Library; Planet Earth Pictures. **34, 35:** Planet Earth Pictures – Alain Compost/Still Pictures; Truchet-Unep/Still Pictures. **37:** Alain Compost/Bruce Coleman Ltd. – Planet Earth Pictures. **38, 39:** Planet Earth Pictures; Gerard & Margi Moss/Still Pictures. **41:** NOAA. **42, 43:** MC Picture Library; CNES, 1987 Distribution Spot Image/Science Photo Library. **44, 45:** Hutchison Library; Paul Harrison/Still Pictures. **46, 47:** George Bernard/Science Photo Library; Hutchison Library. **48, 49:** Planet Earth Pictures; NASA. **50, 51:** Hutchison Library – Bojan Brecelj/Still Pictures; Pete Oxford/Oxford Scientific Films. **53:** NOAA (2). **54, 55:** MC Picture Library (2); Hutchison Library; Planet Earth Pictures. **56, 57:** Planet Earth Pictures; Hutchison Library (2).